The Uncomfortable

Dedicated to 'La Souris'

ISBN-13:
978-1517507534

ISBN-10:
1517507537

Alter native

An age that's getting older
The young maturing fast
With hair a precedent of the old
Clothes wrinkled by the past
Slender men with hourly curves
A time of change in our lives
Ladies and gentlemen, drum roll please
Wholesale gender change arrives
A nation plugged in to beat and sound
Who's running and who is not?
Greedy hands mounting and hearts harden fast
Culture begins to clot

Berserker

Refuelling now for a fierce two-day stint
The battle will commence
Sharpened tools and gaining might
Alas for now it's just a hint
For now it's just a hint

With Nordic charm, with once latent wit
I'm marching down the hillside
Having drank my fill and drank my lot
The drum now steers me on
My drum now steers me on

I've come to claim what it is I love
The weary now lay around
Ruthlessness oozes from the pores
The valiant few rise above
The valiant few rise above

Let go of my hand don't hold me down
This dream is wearing thin
As steel sounds cease the vale clears
The sacrifice as we calm down
My sacrifice as we calm down

Autocracy

We're all plugged in through sight and sound
With the ostensible freedom of choice
Decisions made in our routine
Distinctiveness cannot be found
To break away we follow a style
It seems inescapable to me
The women of zeros and six packs of men
A nation of judgment wholly
Turning the pages of the blood red media
The ink seeps into fingertips
Into hands and up into arms
Installing fear and hysteria
Our boys at the front are surrounded now
No 'Tally ho!' or 'Back to Blighty!'
Were there Allied War crimes in World War two?
If only for 'Internet almighty'

Cambridge

There are scholars and there are squalors
And there is us crammed tight in between
The mediocre majority
The mode, medium and mean

Spoilt for choice

Barista Brevé me!   No make that a short shot in the
dark
Skinny split whipless

                    That's what I like – isn't it?

Bell-bottoms, tracksuit bottoms
         What do you think suits this bottom?
               Hipsters, jeans, pedal-pushers
                    Slacks, sweats, shorts

Make the right food decisions
                 Or does it really matter?

Why make 'Taste the difference'?
            Is the rest 'Simply Substandard?'

Must be ethical, must be methodical
            Range of price, too much choice

Paralysis rather than liberation
            I'm beginning to lose my voice

Oh shit! I've done it again
                It's not perfect
This Pyrenean rosehip jam does not complement harvest grain bread

Who can tame Britain?

By day the city is a nature reserve, untouched, undisturbed
But as darkness descends the creatures come to life
The keepers have packed up for the night
Uncontrollable, unimpeded and wild ensues
Clamouring through beat of wings
Moths circle round lights
Motionless, undetectable by day
Stupefied by the dazzle, by the night
Sharks surface from the depths
Showing teeth, metallic fins glint by their sides
Intent on view, standing by they wait
For a sniff of blood in the air
Later on, helpless small fry flip and flap
In drunken pools gulping for air
Diluted sense, they climb into cabs
Into the arms of the raptorial 'One-nighter'
Walking by the lonely fat toads, in windows they sit
Content with their lack of ambition, with life
One hand on their remotes the other on their hearts,
Scratching arses, sitting in armchairs – steadfast
Hypnotised snakes eating their own tails
Nests made in doorways
Cardboard box wet, almost a paste
Bereft of capital, in a land of capital unwisely placed

Trench warfare

Behind painful pleasantries and feint wry smiles
The elephant in full battle attire looks on from the corner of the room
Each continuing as though nothing has happened
Each fortifying their trench for the emotional conflict
All *is* quiet on the Western Front as the day marches on
Rations get thinner on each side
Who will be the first to surrender?
Will they sign a treaty, as others have done before?
A waste of time uttering Why? Why? Why?
For each other they chose to ignore.
Then he emerges slowly from the trench
In his hand an olive branch
A snapshot from behind sees both figures one approaching the other
Behind her back she is clasping a knife as she marshals him nearer
It's not the first time that she has plunged this into him, will it be the last?
In her mind she has done the right thing and the people behind her agree
She turns to her people, they all cheer
But this is only one side of the line
Unmoved by her actions she continues her policy and she always will
To fight another war with someone new.

The secret

I'm keeping a secret for both of us
Though you wouldn't have a clue
The whisper of minds resonate
My pulse from me to you
The intonation of my soul
Lay my cadence onto you
Out of touch, way out of time
I'm willing to alter mine.

Sleeping Bag

I stayed behind when you went away
Waiting to be back with you, beside you
In limitless warmth, warmth made over the years
The place where I feel completely safe
You made a space for me and you let me in
The pain is lifted with all the complications that time has dealt
The zip is open and you lay there still
I can hear our favourite song playing softly in the milieu
You lay there content gently breathing
I put my arm across your chest to let you know I'm here
You squeeze my hand to gesture
Letting me know all the things you feel
Tucked up together in our tranquil cocoon
Laying together in seamless embrace
I look forward to tender moments
Constant highs and effortless joy
Let's go back to our youth, let's court again
Our first kiss, the dance at the village hall
Live out the memories that we have collected over the years
Happy once more, crying joyous tears

CB1 to NE where but here

Our journeys used to be so fun
But that's now out of view
Knees once touching as we sat in our seats
Pressed together by the sweat of the sun
Eyes absorbing the racing scenery
Preoccupied by the colours and shapes
But now we look jaded seeking out something new
Our love's a crossword puzzle with no numbers and no clues
Once upon a time silence meant contentment
But now all I hear is static and smell the stale air
Return ticket in my hand, one-way in yours
Surrounding yourself with bag after bag
I bring out my pack of cards
But you don't like card games
And you hate the tricks I know
A ruse, a ploy that you've perfected: the blame game
The essence of aspiration for you is to create and then destroy
On your own steam, own materials, own tools, direction and choice
How can I stop this journey when you're driving it so well?
How can I stop this journey when you have created a private hell?

Timelines

No photos could ever capture
The moments, our perfect stills
Exquisite, outstanding, wonderful
In every single way
You will always be my best friend
For twenty thousand and nine hundred days
My face is a photo scrapbook
Of joyful memories
The contour lines are the smiles
And the laughs that we shared
Frown lines fights and arguments
But even then they were times that we cared
And clouds will shape and pass with storms
Lines deepen with our feelings more defined
Two faces from millions
But we are a different kind

I see you, can you see me?

I got high on your reaction
When my pressed lips drew away
You pretended you weren't looking
But I'd rather not know just in case you didn't
You are the compulsion that never quells
But I have now found a new drug, battling
And it's not you
I see you, can you see me?

Glass

We never mean to break glass
But we all manage to at some time

And as it falls
                    It pauses
                    Then crashes on the floor

Joy is wiped clean away from your mouth
                    Replaced by the instant splash, the feeling of dread
                    If only you'd paid more attention

No matter how hard you try the pieces are just too fine
And can never   be pieced together   by effort or by time

Stuck on you

'I want us to be together forever'
The words that she uttered to me
So for months and months I thought of ways
To display the significance of you me and we
So I took her on her word with a commitment oh so true
I bound us together tightly with industrial strength glue
Our anniversary night while she was sleeping
I cradled her in my arms
Pulling back the duvet to see her womanly charms
With a bottle of resin in one hand
More suited for binding wood
I 'went to work' tool belt in tow and did the best I could
'What the hell have you done?'
As she tried to wriggle from the bed
And to my delight I punched the air
The bottle doing exactly what it said, on the tin
After an awkward morning of sighs, hisses and manoeuvring
We formed the glue coalition and combined we did Hoovering
After a while we became accustomed
To synthetic Siamese twins
We customised our clothes
Joined at arm and chest
She made a four-armed cardigan
Elastic waist trousers and a two-headed vest
We now save money on entrance fees
And journeys on the train
And the close proximity means
Sex is on the brain
Making love shapes morning, noon and night
Made our romance ever more watertight
'You wash me and I wash you
So many crevices for us to do'
Drying 'ourself' with a bright green beach towel
Everything seems so summery
But fear of separation plagues my mind
And when she's asleep I top up the bind

Guide to accepting the news of your spouse, partner or lover leaving you

Step 1:
Face the deliverer of news. Rotate your body slightly
While keeping your head straight towards their face
For a woman make sure one foot is positioned behind and slightly diagonal to the front foot
Stand up straight and keep your arms relaxed at your sides
This length and rotation shapes a nice silhouette
A last ditch effort to change their mind
Men should face up head on, looking big and masculine
Again a last ditch effort to change their mind
Step 2:
Make eye contact with the deliverer
Try to project some intensity, focusing on one spot so as to not look dazed
Too much intensity is terrifying – avoid this at all costs
Step 3:
Smile naturally, or as naturally as possible
Flex the muscles below the lips slightly to widen your smile
And tighten your otherwise slack chin
No one likes a slack chin
Smile through your cheekbones as if you do not have a care in the world
Widen the eyes simultaneously so that you avoid squinting
No one likes a squinter
Step 4:
Think of something pleasant or enjoyable as you take the news
Is something totally expected classed as news?
You want to appear earnestly happy, care free, gracious, grown up
Warning and tips: If you are having trouble smiling naturally
Laugh slightly to give your smile an organic look
Avoid too much laughter
Otherwise the deliverer will be reminded of your potent irrational behaviour
This is to be avoided at all costs
Try practicing in front of the mirror
It helps

Black tie event

The black tie hangs waiting
On the rail at the back of the wardrobe
A coating of dust brushed off ready for duty
Care of duty for the times we say goodbye one last time
The uniform of sad farewells drawing the curtain once more
The black tie hangs over blackened hearts
As the shadow of the family tree extends its reach
Haunted by memories, happy and sad
Some go happy, some go before their time
Although stretched it's never enough
But we can all be greedy sometimes
Love is time's accomplice committing the greatest crime

Disassembling hearts

Secrets should remain secret
No exceptions to the rule
But if there is a time to know, it's now
Is this shared secret the one to rue?
Its perfection in this hazy romp of lust
But you must know the allure will soon fade
So make sure when you do love me for me
It's not illusion, apparent, everything you see
And I will soon change in fits and starts
Plus I'll let you down in gradual parts
It's how its starts, it's how its starts
Disassembling hearts
I'll drink when I'm feeling just a little down
But I will worship the earth, the very ground
You'll be standing on; I'm at your feet
Pathetically perhaps or does this make me sweet?
But there's something *you* need to know about me
I worry how I look and sound
And how I'm meant to be
You're the depicter of relationships perfectly
It's me that will always expect the fall
Disappointment haunts me with her familiar call
Emotional dysfunctional tarnished by strain
But it wouldn't be right to not feel the rain
Then let's 'put it there', work a way from the maze
And be prepared when we slip out of this faze
Don't expect much, no fairy-tale sweep
Let's stand poised ready on our own two feet

Si Garetta

Si, Garetta she is beautiful
Unrelenting cool, fashionable always
standing with the crowd, expensive taste
Though a taste you need to get used to
And after a while you are hooked
Not looked upon as a picture of health
Or wealth as time slips by
Her looks fade and the money dwindles
She starts her slow suffocating
Of everything you used to be
She is too much, si, Garetta
Fun for a while, terminal for her style

Real man

Am I real man if I show my emotions?
Am I a real man if I lack sexual prowess?
Am I a real man for not having a granite chiselled 'Y' shape physique?
I don't take my top off at the faintest glimpse of the sun
Am I a real man if I don't like cars, motorbikes or driving fast?
If I like to go to the doctor's for a check-up now and again
And what if I cannot undo a bra strap with one hand?
Or don't find pornography especially arousing
I prefer a woman of mind, intellect and forward thinking?
To a woman predacious with intercourse, with hands forward sinking
I don't like the great outdoors, fishing
Hunting, camping, or universal danger for that matter
Am I a real man if I don't carry a big bunch of keys?
Have limited spatial navigation skills
Prefer wine to beer, ale or shots
I don't think I want to be a real man

The Oracle

If this drink is my escape
Then warden chain me to the wall
'Have another', he utters
But it is this that will take us all
For the noxious thoughts I contain
Become the toxic words I'll share
The bottle is my mouthpiece
To play my awful song
Words to my love, slurred as they tempt
The baited quarrel poetry that I never dared
Speak to me Co-dependent!

I'm right here by your side
For your whack of voluntary madness
No one will keep me dry
Not even you, no, no, no never
No matter how much you cry
Cry all you like see if I care
You don't love me or even understand
But when I wake you lay there
Empty, hollowed, holding my hand.

Only happy in the now

Sometimes just a small pipette, a droplet of thought
Is enough to break the tank of resistance
Resistance to the idea that we
Are all on the same road
That there's a start to this journey
And there's and end
We are all scrambling nail deep
To do the best with the time in between
One end to the other
Why worry about the linier?
The 'what' could happen
The 'may' never happen
And the 'won't' happen
So what?
Happiness emerges from your freedoms
The do as you please
Emphasis on the 'please'
As you will find that if you do not please yourself
How can you please others?
Contentment lies poised pious in all of us
But contentment is an immediate creature
Only happy in the now

The Circle

I am the circle
Rotund and seemingly pointless
Nothing much to offer
Look at me from another angle
You see me just 2D don't you
But if you took time to interact
Not just take me from face value
You will see that I have more to offer
I have an ability of coping with problems
I simply roll away
Stopping is more difficult
When no one will give you the time of day

Little grown up

On a cold January evening
Came the hour of misuse
Unwitting I was called to
The room to amuse
And as the air of the room
Brushed my immature skin
And in the chair was my tutor
Sporting an ambiguous grin
Was it a game of plain pleasure?
Or just for clandestine thrill
Minute-hand never moved
When he cheated my will

Cinematic Steven

Scene 1

Cinematic Steven plays out many roles
Never a lead role or a small talking part
The middle-aged, middle of the road man of
Meritocracy gone mad, hiding amongst the extras
Crowding his mind with shrieks and solicited screams
In an antiquated theatre he dreams up the odd and the strange
Playing out fantasies, enacting
Horror, fortune about to change
Locked in one night, a sweet twist of fate
Hidden away in the projector room until completely still
Parched, he drinks the gifts left, of half full cola cups
And gorges on the scraps of popcorn left in bags on the floor
Half nourished by his midnight feast he creeps around the old projector room
Making a bed of celluloid he prepares for his new role
Unable to sleep he works the projector watching
Stephen King films he forgets to watch his soul
Between the years of 1992 and 2001 Steven watched them all
Reruns of Jaws, classic thrillers, slashers and all the latest pictures
But Cinematic felt safer with horror, filled with gratification
But he turned his attention to the audiences, the payers
Watching the tiers, faces transfixed, transformed, exposing their fears
Recipes of sharp held strings, gore and struggling women
Knives slashing in the dark, steely cries, helpless tears
This is his showcase, jubilant as a witness, desperate for reviews

Scene 2

'Cinematic' lays in wait in the narrow lobby
Pouncing on the payers desperate for reaction and reports
'Did that scare you?' 'Wasn't that great?'
Howling for more, but reactions are mixed, hounded
Puncturing his frame with disappointment
He disappears into the darkness. Wounded
Time passes in two-hour slots, day after day
Skin pales, no retort with synthetic light, short shrift
Eyes bulbous, mind torsion
But as fate twists again, an unrequited gesture
Spills into conversation, something more than before
He follows her down through the double door
Pausing for a moment, his first lung fill of natural city air
Gentle drizzle moistening every exposed pore
Into a pastiche of Tim Burton's Gotham City
Everything in black and white
Black oil pits disturbed shining in the haunted moonlight
The pavement and walls reflect like metallic panels
Wendy was thirty yards ahead
Wherever she was walking to I knew I didn't have long
Soft violins Staccato with intent
Then Viola and cello like sawing throng
In a frenzied swipe I pull Wendy to the ground
Smothering her, waiting for my director to shout cut
Struggling she kicks free against my weakened arms
Shouting as I fall and crack my head
The cold winter's puddle begins to feel warm
I slip helplessly into a dream
Floating down my own inflicted red carpet stream...
No premiere for 'Cinematic' in the damp pale walled cell
Next prison, then the madhouse and then the grave
A method movie star until the end, 'Cinematic' plays his part
But no Hollywood Boulevard, just the graveyard

Underwater swimming

I love swimming under water
Sinking under the waterline and

Pushing off the side
Gliding as most hydro dynamically possible
Until I slow to a submerged weightless standstill
I love the cool blue surrounding
It's a shame I can't breathe in there
It's a short term escape, silent paradise
No objects of desire, just air

Chopper

I buried her this morning
In the moments before the light
At the end of the garden behind the shrubs
Beneath the cement pervaded dirt
With no adjacent wasteland to conceal my action
To conceal this grotesque crime
Dismantled and bagged with no telltale shape to
This dear sweet love of mine
The coast was clear, and I rolled her out
On the day they could have taken her
But to my horror, to my dismay, there she still remained
Slumped by the fence still wrapped up tight
They must have known! They must have seen!
With no time to lose I clambered down the alley
Picked up the remnants with both fouled hands
I scuttled back to rethink my plan

That night the spirit souls disturbed me
The bubble of thought bursting before resolution
I could see my love's body clearly and then she uttered to me
My brain hummed numbed distilled invention and decay
The hours we had shared touching so intimately
Boiling with no vent, condensation dripping back in
Pedalling back and forth our passion and love
Outer pressure controlled by my lack of expression
So many places we saw and all only possible through one other
Ardent angst evaporates as relativity can equate
Scheme and design amalgamate
Time to rollout this fate

So, I buried her this morning
In the moments before the light
At the end of the garden behind the shrubs
Beneath the cement pervaded dirt
With no adjacent wasteland to conceal my action
To conceal this grotesque crime
Dismantled and bagged with no tell-tale shape to
This dear sweet love of mine
So why do I pay my taxes?
For flaky political will- monopolised?
Lack of robust council schemes that fail to penalised the unjust?
Partisan, why do you refuse my refuse?
Come forth the filth, filth pile higher
So that the cats are fat, and those filthy rats can remain amused

Simplicity of life

The night is made of dots and black
You're awake and then you're not
You work you eat you walk and talk
Child, teens, love and then you're old
You die and that's your lot.

Our Selfish Gene

Am I selfish? Or is it you?
Martial world states, opposing moral views
Cardinal quality in our nature
Surfacing from primordial stew
Labelling the good and labelling the bad
Separation from the other creatures
Instinct or formative learning?
Praise for the selfish gene – we are so glad
Player 'A' versus Player 'B'
Implicate your friend to be set free
Man has evolved; all are armour clad
For every sexual encounter you will have or ever had

And what another flipside? We *do* collaborate
Daily risks through blinded trust
Credulous attitude to the traffic lights
Flying with foreign aerodynamic thrust
The doctor's prognosis, education we are taught
Is who built your car a question you should really give a thought?
Words and language wonders, such astonishing acts and feats
From a complicated tearful parting to a simple facial greet
Without altruism things would be different, much different to how we know it
There's a seed planted for empathy, with the hardest task to show it
Our own self-interest is often matched by unrelenting shame
And this is you this is meant for you, the pervasive morally lame

What wasps are for

You shooed me out of the door once more
I heard you turn the key
Unkind until the end
Your subtle well timed gestures

With my back to you I felt the warmth
But not exuded from your affection
Just the air escaped forced into the cold
A pale moment of reflection

You wore yellow and black most of the time
Which firmly reflected your nature
I always danced around your physical sweetness
But you have always been only half beautiful

When I stop making you paper nests
You'll wake and see much more
Put your teleology to one side
And you'll discover what wasps are for

13968335R00020

Printed in Great Britain
by Amazon.co.uk, Ltd.,
Marston Gate.